PIANO • VOCAL • GUITAR

ULTIMATE
BROADWAY
PLATINUM

•100 FAVORITE SHOW TUNES•

ISBN 0-7935-4324-X

HAL•LEONARD®
CORPORATION
7777 W. BLUEMOUND RD. P.O. BOX 13819 MILWAUKEE, WI 53213

Visit Hal Leonard Online at
www.halleonard.com

PIANO • VOCAL • GUITAR

•100 FAVORITE SHOW TUNES•

ANY DREAM WILL DO

from JOSEPH AND THE AMAZING TECHNICOLOR® DREAMCOAT

Music by ANDREW LLOYD WEBBER
Lyrics by TIM RICE

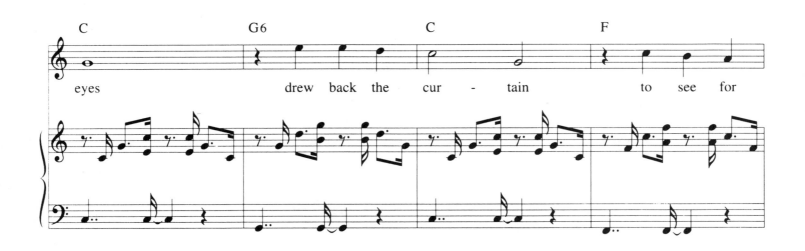

way   some - one was weep - ing,   but the world was

sleep - ing,   a - ny dream will   do.   I wore my

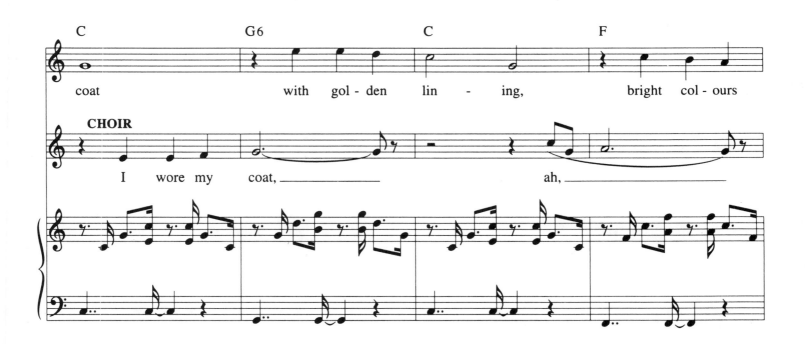

coat   with gol - den lin - ing,   bright col - ours

CHOIR

I wore my coat, _____ ah, _____

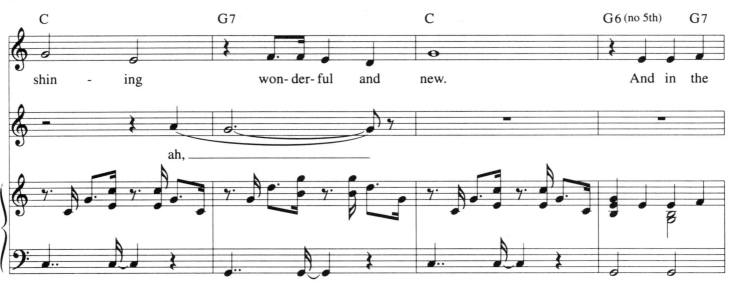

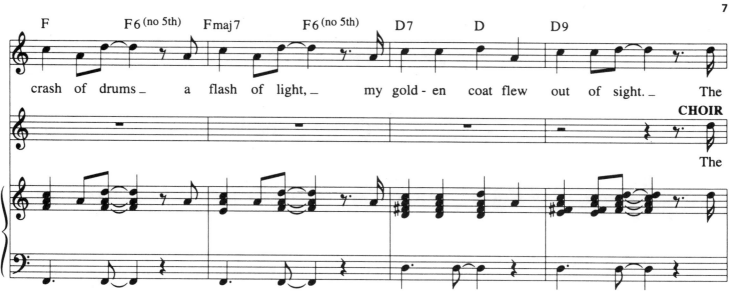

crash of drums _ a flash of light, _ my gold-en coat flew out of sight. _ The

The

col-ours fad-ed in-to dark-ness, I was left a-lone. _____

col-ours fad-ed in-to dark-ness, ah, _____ ah, _____

ah. _____ May I re-turn, to the be-

May I re-turn,

- gin - ning, the light is dim - ming and the dream is
ah, _____ ah. _____

too, the world and I, we are still
The world and I, _____

wait - ing, still he - si - ta - ting a - ny dream will
ah, _____ ah. _____

AS IF WE NEVER SAID GOODBYE

from SUNSET BOULEVARD

Music by ANDREW LLOYD WEBBER
Lyrics by DON BLACK
and CHRISTOPHER HAMPTON,
with contributions by AMY POWERS

can't know how_ I've missed you,_____ missed the fai-ry tale ad-ven-tures___ in this

ev-er-spin-ning play - ground.__ We were young to - geth - er, I'm

com-ing out of make-up, the light's al-rea-dy burn-ing,___ not long un-til_ the

cam-eras will_ start turn - ing,_____ and the ear-ly morn-ing mad - ness,_

AS LONG AS HE NEEDS ME

from the Broadway Musical OLIVER!

Words and Music by
LIONEL BART

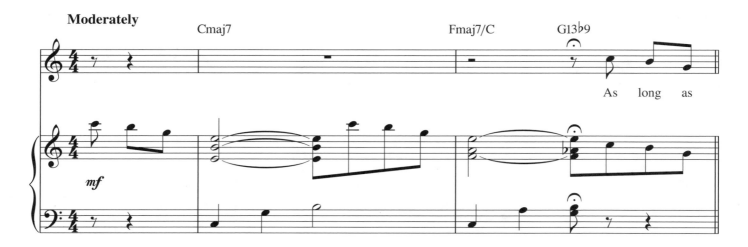

he needs me _____ I know where I must be, _____ I'll cling on
life is long, _____ I'll love him, right or wrong; _____ and some-how

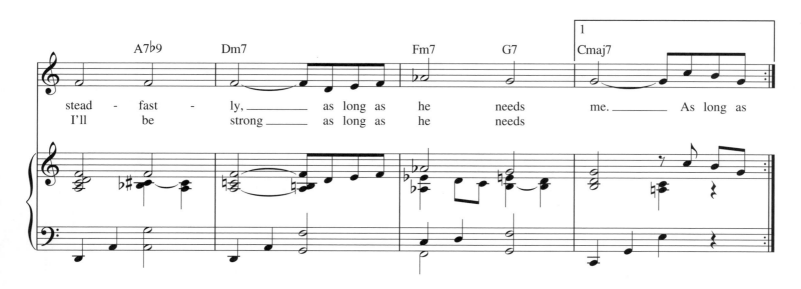

stead - fast - ly, _____ as long as he needs me. _____ As long as
I'll be strong _____ as long as he needs

BALI HA'I

from SOUTH PACIFIC

Lyrics by OSCAR HAMMERSTEIN II
Music by RICHARD RODGERS

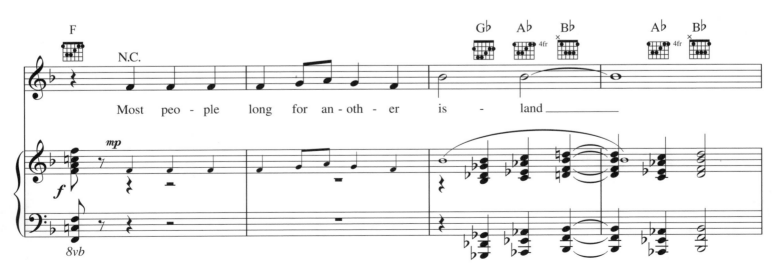

THE BLUE ROOM
from THE GIRL FRIEND

Words by LORENZ HART
Music by RICHARD RODGERS

BEAUTY AND THE BEAST

from Walt Disney's BEAUTY AND THE BEAST: THE BROADWAY MUSICAL

Lyrics by HOWARD ASHMAN
Music by ALAN MENKEN

THE BEST THINGS IN LIFE ARE FREE

from GOOD NEWS!

Music and Lyrics by B.G. DeSYLVA,
LEW BROWN and RAY HENDERSON

BYE BYE BIRDIE

from BYE BYE BIRDIE

Lyric by LEE ADAMS
Music by CHARLES STROUSE

CABARET
from the Musical CABARET

Words by FRED EBB
Music by JOHN KANDER

38

CAMELOT
from CAMELOT

Words by ALAN JAY LERNER
Music by FREDERICK LOEWE

Moderato

Refrain (tempo guisto)

A law was made a dis-tant moon a-go here_____ Ju-ly and Au-gust

can-not be too hot; And there's a le-gal lim-it to the

snow here_____ In Cam-e-lot. The

CLIMB EV'RY MOUNTAIN
from THE SOUND OF MUSIC

Lyrics by OSCAR HAMMERSTEIN II
Music by RICHARD RODGERS

Maestoso

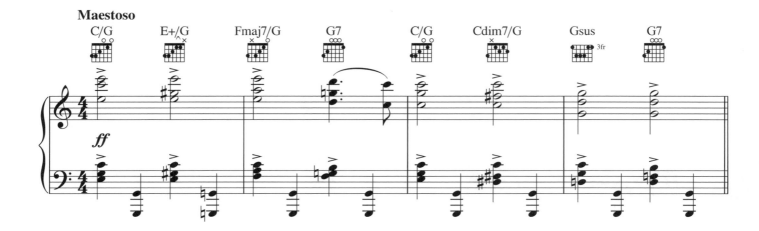

Refrain (*with deep feeling, like a prayer*)

Climb ev - 'ry moun - tain, search high and low,

Fol - low ev - 'ry by - way, ev - 'ry path you know.

CONSIDER YOURSELF

from the Broadway Musical OLIVER!

Words and Music by
LIONEL BART

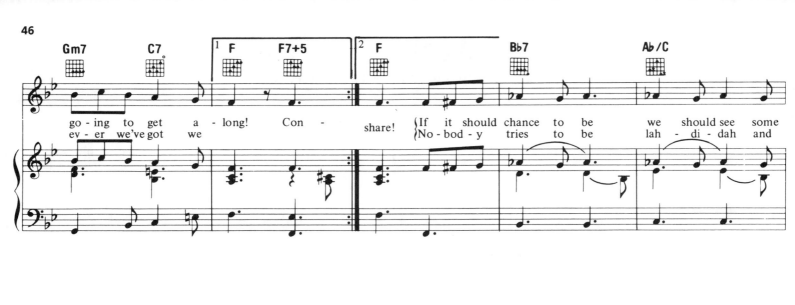

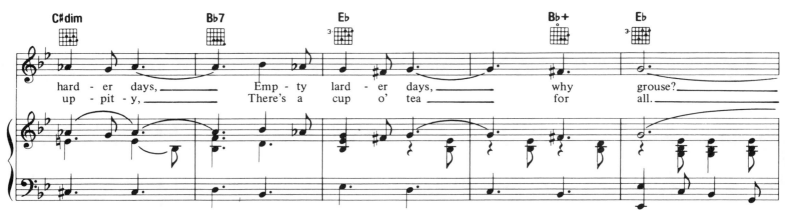

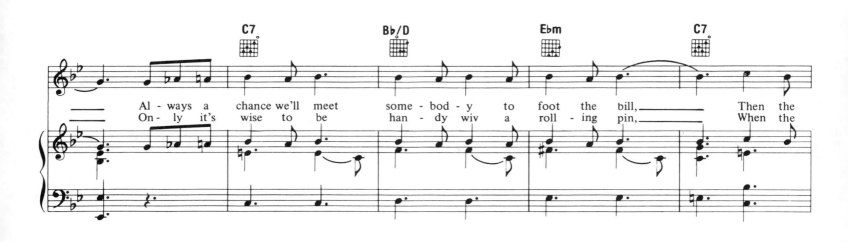

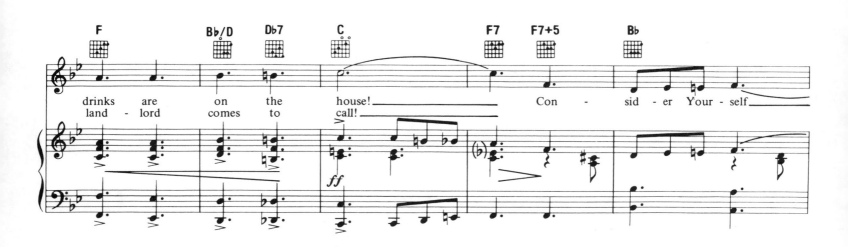

DAY BY DAY
from the Musical GODSPELL

Words and Music by
STEPHEN SCHWARTZ

50

DO YOU HEAR THE PEOPLE SING?

from LES MISÉRABLES

Music by CLAUDE-MICHEL SCHÖNBERG
Lyrics by ALAIN BOUBLIL, JEAN-MARC NATEL
and HERBERT KRETZMER

DON'T RAIN ON MY PARADE

from FUNNY GIRL

Words by BOB MERRILL
Music by JULE STYNE

57

EVERYTHING'S COMING UP ROSES

from GYPSY

Words by STEPHEN SONDHEIM
Music by JULE STYNE

ELABORATE LIVES

from Walt Disney Theatrical Productions' AIDA

Music by ELTON JOHN
Lyrics by TIM RICE

FALLING IN LOVE WITH LOVE

from THE BOYS FROM SYRACUSE

Words by LORENZ HART
Music by RICHARD RODGERS

FROM THIS MOMENT ON

from OUT OF THIS WORLD

Words and Music by
COLE PORTER

GET ME TO THE CHURCH ON TIME

from MY FAIR LADY

Words by ALAN JAY LERNER
Music by FREDERICK LOEWE

GUS: THE THEATRE CAT

from CATS

Music by ANDREW LLOYD WEBBER
Text by T.S. ELIOT

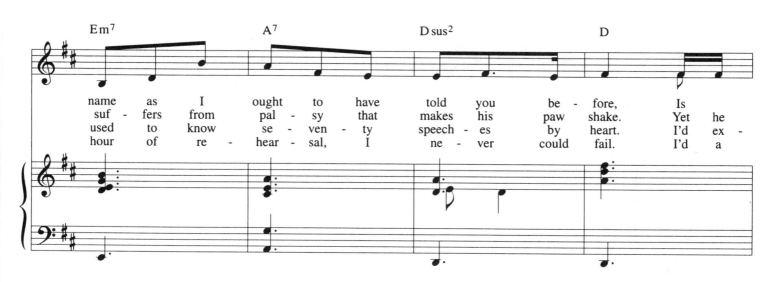

Gus is the Cat at the The-a-tre Door. His
coat's ve-ry shab-by, he's thin as a rake, And he
played, in my time, eve-ry pos-si-ble part And I
knew how to act with my back and my tail; With an

name as I ought to have told you be-fore, Is
suf-fers from pal-sy that makes his paw shake. Yet he
used to know se-ven-ty speech-es by heart. I'd ex-
hour of re-hear-sal, I ne-ver could fail. I'd a

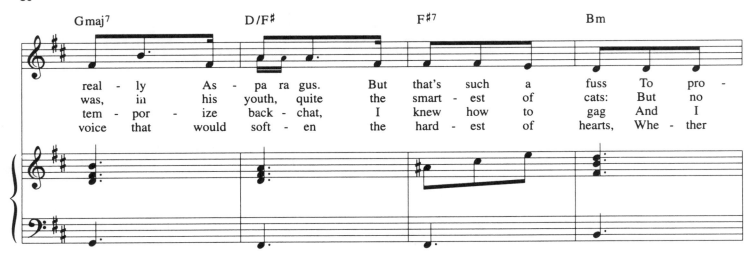

real - ly As - pa ra gus. But that's such a fuss To pro -
was, in his youth, quite the smart - est of cats: But no
tem - por - ize back - chat, I knew how to gag And I
voice that would soft - en the hard - est of hearts, Whe - ther

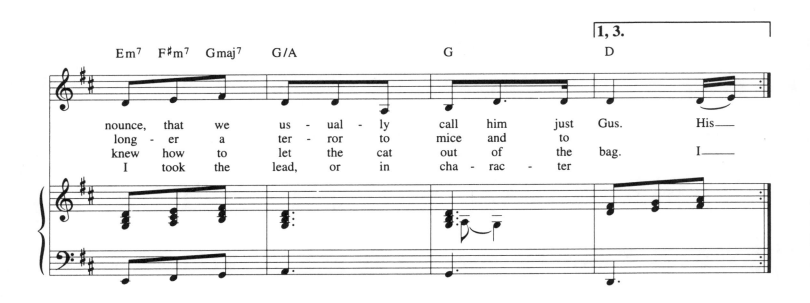

1, 3.

nounce, that we us - ual - ly call him just Gus. His___
long - er a ter - ror to mice and just to
knew how to let the cat out of the bag. I___
I took the lead, or in cha - rac - ter

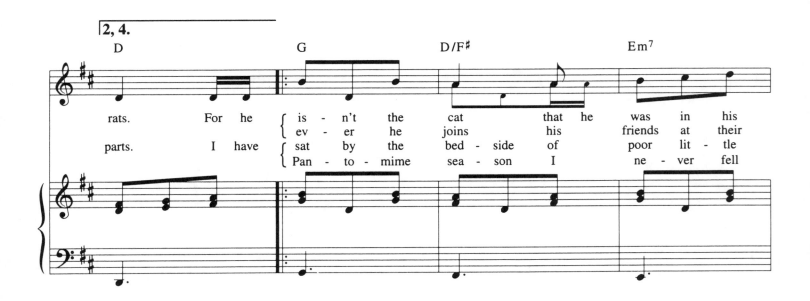

2, 4.

rats. For he { is - n't the cat that he was in his
{ ev - er he joins his friends at their
parts. I have { sat by the bed - side of poor lit - tle
{ Pan - to - mime sea - son I ne - ver fell

4° *To Coda* ⊕ 1, 3.

prime; Though his name was quite fa - mous, he says, in his time. And when
club (Which takes place at the back of the neigh - bour - ing
Nell; When the cur - few was rung, then I swung on the bell. In the
flat, and I once un - der - stu - died Dick Whit - ting - ton's

2.

pub.) He loves to re - gale them, if some - one else pays, With

an - ec - dotes drawn from his palm - i - est days. For he

once was a Star of the high - est de - gree: He has act - ed with
likes to re - late his suc - cess on the Halls, Where the Gal - le - ry

GUS (Sung reprise)
And I once crossed the stage on a telegraph wire,
To rescue a child when a house was on fire.
And I think that I still can much better than most,
Produced blood-curdling noises to bring on the Ghost.
I once played Growltiger, could do it again…

GETTING TO KNOW YOU
from THE KING AND I

Lyrics by OSCAR HAMMERSTEIN II
Music by RICHARD RODGERS

89

GIGI
from GIGI

Words by ALAN JAY LERNER
Music by FREDERICK LOEWE

GONNA BUILD A MOUNTAIN

from the Musical Production STOP THE WORLD—I WANT TO GET OFF

Words and Music by LESLIE BRICUSSE
and ANTHONY NEWLEY

93

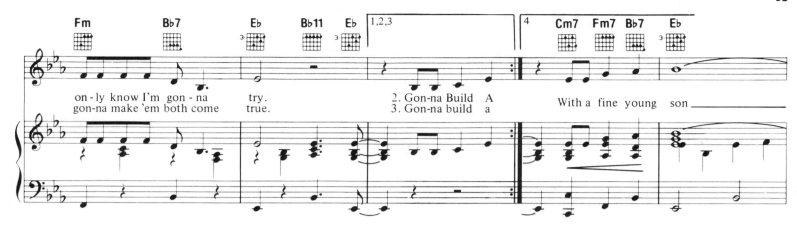

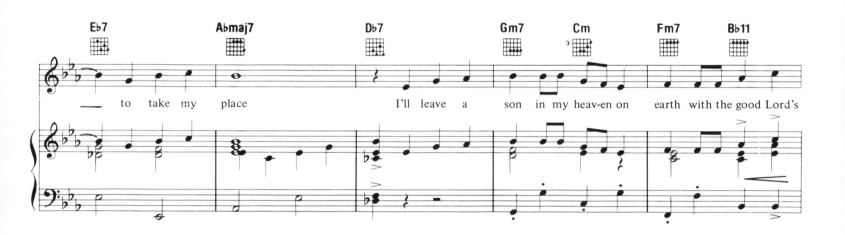

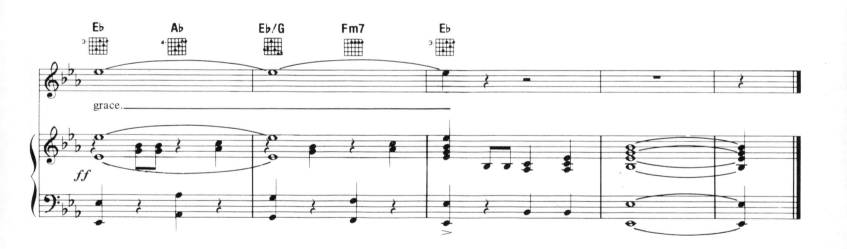

Verse 3. Gon-na build a heaven from a little hell.
Gon-na build a heaven and I know darn well.
If I build my mountain with a lot of care.
And take my daydream up the mountain heaven
will be waiting there.

Verse 4. When I've built that heaven as I will some day
And the Lord sends Gabriel to take me away,
Wanna fine young son to take my place
I'll leave a son in my heav-en on earth,
With the Lord's good grace.

HABEN SIE GEHÖRT DAS DEUTSCHE BAND?
(Have You Ever Heard the German Band?)
from THE PRODUCERS

Music and Lyrics by
MEL BROOKS

HELLO, YOUNG LOVERS

from THE KING AND I

Lyrics by OSCAR HAMMERSTEIN II
Music by RICHARD RODGERS

Refrain *(very moderately)*

103

HOW ARE THINGS IN GLOCCA MORRA

from FINIAN'S RAINBOW

Words by E.Y. HARBURG
Music by BURTON LANE

I CONCENTRATE ON YOU

from BROADWAY MELODY OF 1940

Words and Music by
COLE PORTER

I CAN DREAM, CAN'T I?

from RIGHT THIS WAY

Lyric by IRVING KAHAL
Music by SAMMY FAIN

I can see, no mat-ter how near you'll be, You'll nev-er be-

long to me. But I Can Dream, Can't I?

Can't I pre-tend that I'm locked in the bend of your em-brace? For dreams are

I CAN'T GET STARTED WITH YOU

from ZIEGFELD FOLLIES

Words by IRA GERSHWIN
Music by VERNON DUKE

I COULD WRITE A BOOK

from PAL JOEY

Words by LORENZ HART
Music by RICHARD RODGERS

I ENJOY BEING A GIRL

from FLOWER DRUM SONG

Lyrics by OSCAR HAMMERSTEIN II
Music by RICHARD RODGERS

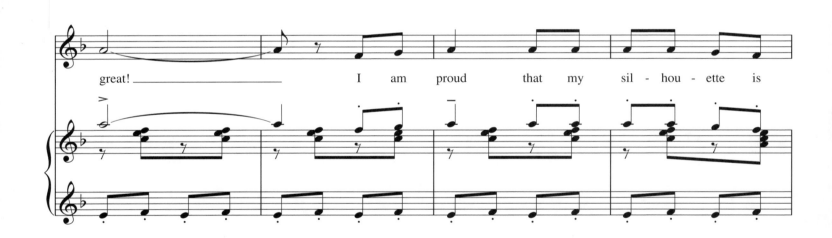

read - y for the race! _____ When

Refrain *(brightly)*

I have a brand new hair - do _____ With my

eye - lash - es all in curl, _____ I

float as the clouds on air do, _____ I en -

I KNOW WHERE I'VE BEEN

from HAIRSPRAY

Music by MARC SHAIMAN
Lyrics by MARC SHAIMAN and SCOTT WITTMAN

I LOVE YOU
from MEXICAN HAYRIDE

Words and Music by
COLE PORTER

I REMEMBER IT WELL

from GIGI

Words by ALAN JAY LERNER
Music by FREDERICK LOEWE

I STILL BELIEVE IN LOVE

from THEY'RE PLAYING OUR SONG

Words by CAROLE BAYER SAGER
Music by MARVIN HAMLISCH

I'VE GOT YOU UNDER MY SKIN

from BORN TO DANCE

Words and Music by
COLE PORTER

I WANNA BE A PRODUCER

from THE PRODUCERS

Music and Lyrics by
MEL BROOKS

LEO:

I wan-na be a pro-duc-er show the

SHOWGIRLS:

Drink cham-pagne till he pukes!

LEO:

world just what I've got I'm gon-na put-on shows _ that will en - thrall _ 'em

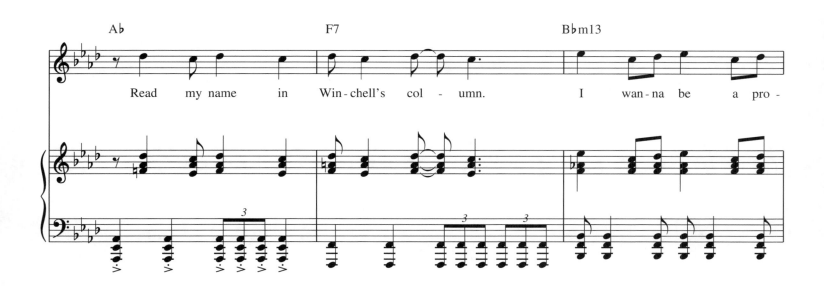

Read my name in Win-chell's col - umn. I wan-na be a pro-

I'LL BE SEEING YOU

from RIGHT THIS WAY

Lyric by IRVING KAHAL
Music by SAMMY FAIN

151

I'M GONNA WASH THAT MAN RIGHT OUTA MY HAIR

from SOUTH PACIFIC

Lyrics by OSCAR HAMMERSTEIN II
Music by RICHARD RODGERS

Don't try to patch it up, Tear it up, tear it up! Wash him out, dry him out,

Push him out, fly him out, Can - cel him and let him

go! Yea, sis - ter! I'm gon - na wash that man right

out - a my hair, I'm gon - na wash that man right out - a my hair, I'm gon - na

I'VE GROWN ACCUSTOMED TO HER FACE

from MY FAIR LADY

Words by ALAN JAY LERNER
Music by FREDERICK LOEWE

IF EVER I WOULD LEAVE YOU

from CAMELOT

Words by ALAN JAY LERNER
Music by FREDERICK LOEWE

IF THIS ISN'T LOVE

from FINIAN'S RAINBOW

Words by E.Y. HARBURG
Music by BURTON LANE

IN THE STILL OF THE NIGHT

from ROSALIE

Words and Music by
COLE PORTER

169

IT MIGHT AS WELL BE SPRING

from STATE FAIR

Lyrics by OSCAR HAMMERSTEIN II
Music by RICHARD RODGERS

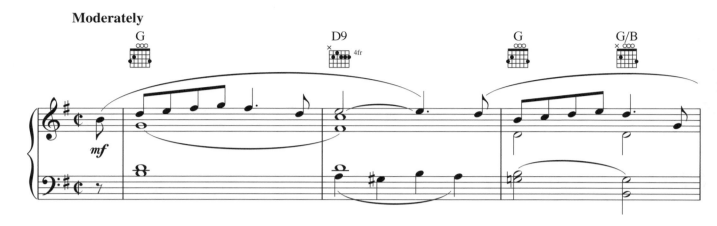

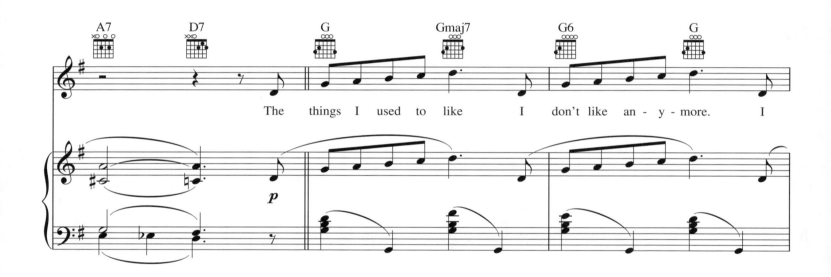

The things I used to like I don't like an-y-more. I

want a lot of oth-er things I've nev-er had be-fore. It's just like moth-er

MAMA, I'M A BIG GIRL NOW

from HAIRSPRAY

Music by MARC SHAIMAN
Lyrics by MARC SHAIMAN and SCOTT WITTMAN

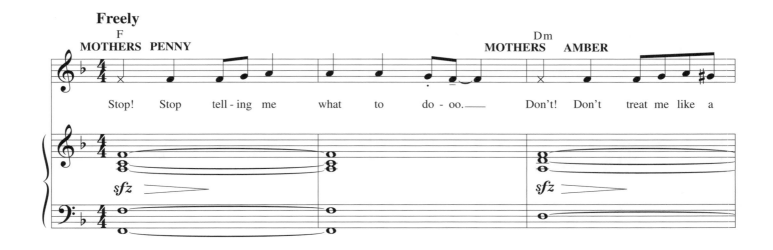

IT'S A GRAND NIGHT FOR SINGING

from STATE FAIR

Lyrics by OSCAR HAMMERSTEIN II
Music by RICHARD RODGERS

Tempo di Valse

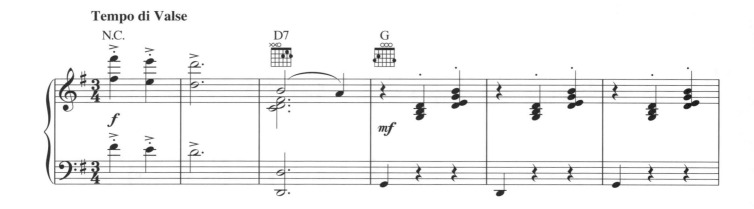

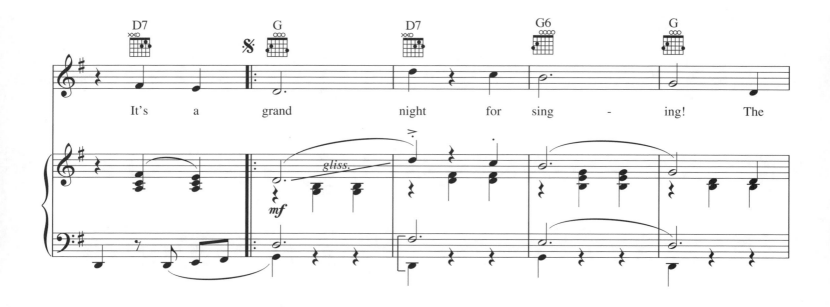

It's a grand night for sing - ing! The

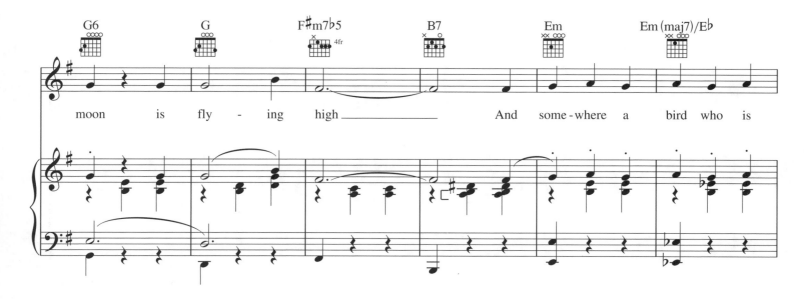

moon is fly - ing high ___ And some-where a bird who is

IT'S DE-LOVELY

from RED, HOT AND BLUE!

Words and Music by
COLE PORTER

189

*Pronounced "delukes"

JUST IN TIME

from BELLS ARE RINGING

Words by BETTY COMDEN
and ADOLPH GREEN
Music by JULE STYNE

LITTLE GIRL BLUE

from JUMBO

Words by LORENZ HART
Music by RICHARD RODGERS

LOOK TO THE RAINBOW

from FINIAN'S RAINBOW

Words by E.Y. HARBURG
Music by BURTON LANE

A LOT OF LIVIN' TO DO
from BYE BYE BIRDIE

Lyric by LEE ADAMS
Music by CHARLES STROUSE

A Lot of Livin' to Do - 4 - 1

MAYBE

from the Musical Production ANNIE

Lyric by MARTIN CHARNIN
Music by CHARLES STROUSE

MR. WONDERFUL

from the Musical MR. WONDERFUL

Words and Music by JERRY BOCK,
LARRY HOLOFCENER and GEORGE DAVID WEISS

Slowly and expressively

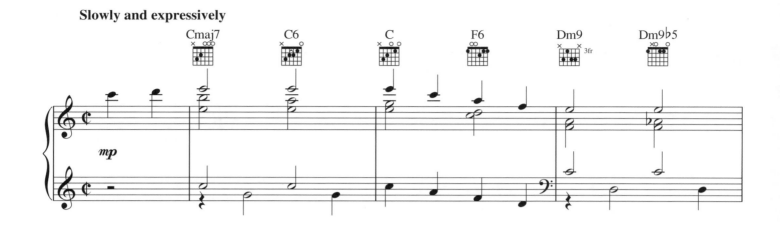

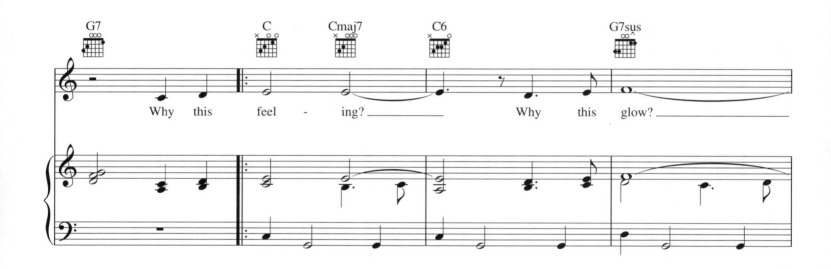

Why this feel - ing? _____ Why this glow? _____

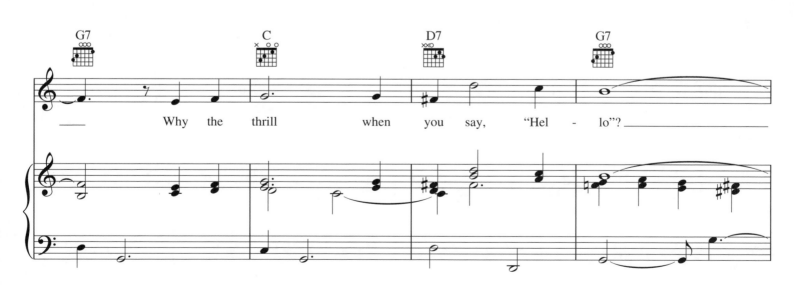

_____ Why the thrill when you say, "Hel - lo"? _____

THE MUSIC OF THE NIGHT
from THE PHANTOM OF THE OPERA

Music by ANDREW LLOYD WEBBER
Lyrics by CHARLES HART
Additional Lyrics by RICHARD STILGOE

Andante

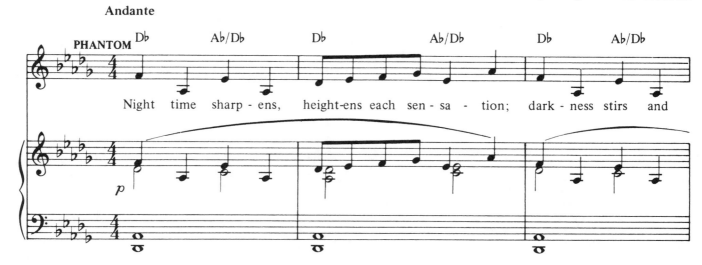

Night time sharp-ens, height-ens each sen-sa - tion; dark-ness stirs and

wakes im-ag-in-a - tion. Si - lent-ly the sen - ses a - ban-don their de-fen - ces.

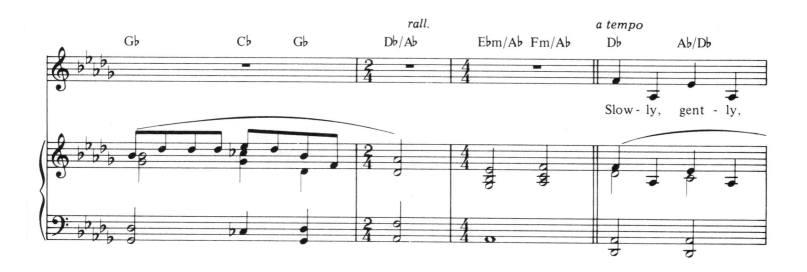

Slow-ly, gent-ly,

eyes let your spi-rit start to soar and you'll live as you've nev-er lived be - fore.

Soft - ly, deft - ly, mu-sic shall ca-ress you. Hear it, feel it,

se - cret - ly po - ssess you. O - pen up your mind let your fan - ta - sies un-wind in this

dark-ness which you know you can - not fight, the dark-ness of the mu-sic of the

MY CUP RUNNETH OVER

from I DO! I DO!

Words by TOM JONES
Music by HARVEY SCHMIDT

OH, WHAT A BEAUTIFUL MORNIN'

from OKLAHOMA!

Lyrics by OSCAR HAMMERSTEIN II
Music by RICHARD RODGERS

Moderate Waltz

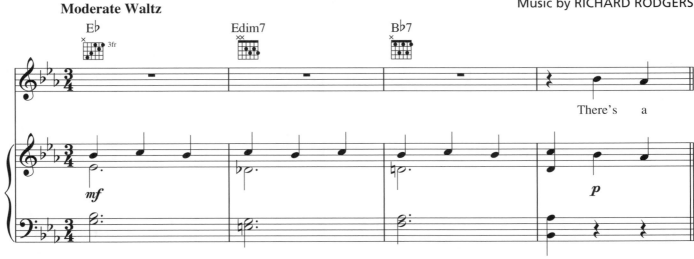

There's a

bright gold-en haze on the mead-ow, ___
cat-tle are stand-in' like stat-ues, ___
sounds of the earth are like mu-sic, ___

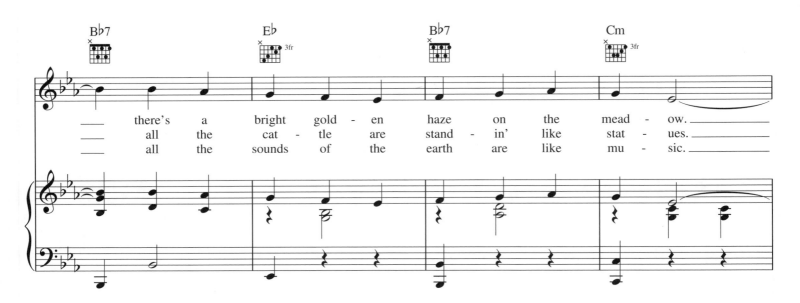

___ there's a bright gold-en haze on the mead-ow. ___
___ all the cat-tle are stand-in' like stat-ues. ___
___ all the sounds of the earth are like mu-sic. ___

MY FAVORITE THINGS

from THE SOUND OF MUSIC

Lyrics by OSCAR HAMMERSTEIN II
Music by RICHARD RODGERS

Girls in white dress - es with blue sat - in sash - es, Snow - flakes that

stay on my nose and eye - lash - es, Sil - ver white win - ters that

melt in - to springs, These are a few of my fa - vor - ite things.

When the dog bites, When the bee stings,

221

MY HEART BELONGS TO DADDY

from LEAVE IT TO ME

Words and Music by
COLE PORTER

NO OTHER LOVE

from ME AND JULIET

Lyrics by OSCAR HAMMERSTEIN II
Music by RICHARD RODGERS

ON A CLEAR DAY
(You Can See Forever)
from ON A CLEAR DAY YOU CAN SEE FOREVER

Words by ALAN JAY LERNER
Music by BURTON LANE

229

ON MY OWN

from LES MISÉRABLES

Music by CLAUDE-MICHEL SCHÖNBERG
Lyrics by ALAIN BOUBLIL, JOHN CAIRD, TREVOR NUNN,
JEAN-MARC NATEL and HERBERT KRETZMER

SEEING IS BELIEVING

from ASPECTS OF LOVE

Music by ANDREW LLOYD WEBBER
Lyrics by DON BLACK
and CHARLES HART

THE PARTY'S OVER

from BELLS ARE RINGING

Words by BETTY COMDEN
and ADOLPH GREEN
Music by JULE STYNE

PEOPLE

from FUNNY GIRL

Words by BOB MERRILL
Music by JULE STYNE

PUT ON A HAPPY FACE

from BYE BYE BIRDIE

Lyric by LEE ADAMS
Music by CHARLES STROUSE

SEPTEMBER SONG

from the Musical Play KNICKERBOCKER HOLIDAY

Words by MAXWELL ANDERSON
Music by KURT WEILL

SMALL WORLD

from GYPSY

Words by STEPHEN SONDHEIM
Music by JULE STYNE

SOMEONE LIKE YOU

from JEKYLL & HYDE

Words by LESLIE BRICUSSE
Music by FRANK WILDHORN

THE SOUND OF MUSIC
from THE SOUND OF MUSIC

Lyrics by OSCAR HAMMERSTEIN II
Music by RICHARD RODGERS

Molto moderato *(tenderly)*

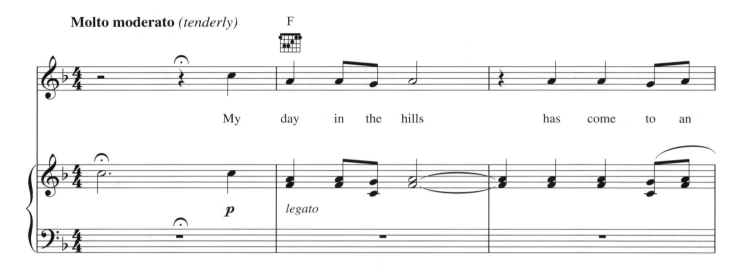

My day in the hills has come to an

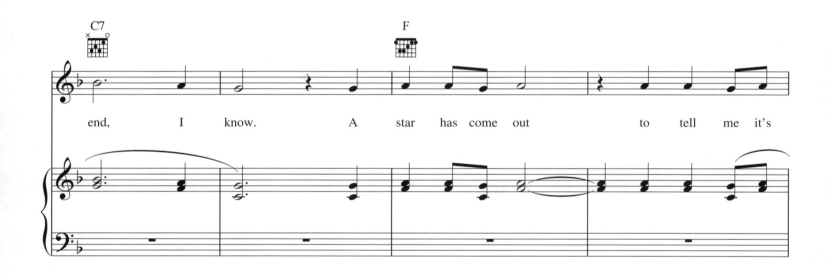

end, I know. A star has come out to tell me it's

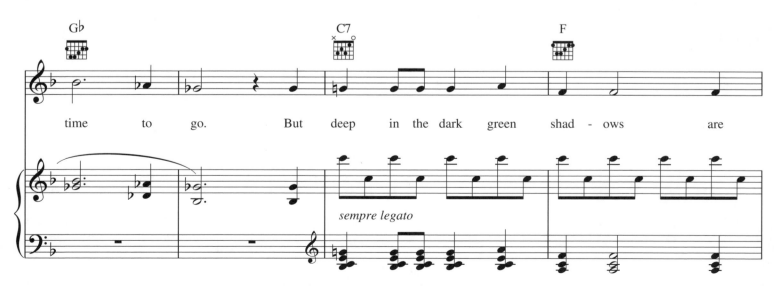

time to go. But deep in the dark green shad-ows are

voic - es that urge me to stay. So I pause and I wait and I

lis - ten for one more sound, For one more love-ly thing that the hills might

Refrain (*moderately, with warm expression*)

say. The hills are a - live with the sound of mu - sic, _____

_____ With songs they have sung for a thou - sand years. _____

256

SPEAK LOW

from the Musical Production ONE TOUCH OF VENUS

Words by OGDEN NASH
Music by KURT WEILL

SUN AND MOON

from MISS SAIGON

Music by CLAUDE-MICHEL SCHÖNBERG
Lyrics by RICHARD MALTBY JR. and ALAIN BOUBLIL
Adapted from original French Lyrics by ALAIN BOUBLIL

Lyrics:

KIM: You are sun-light and I moon, joined by the gods of for-tune, mid-night and high noon shar-ing the sky.

THE SURREY WITH THE FRINGE ON TOP

from OKLAHOMA!

Lyrics by OSCAR HAMMERSTEIN II
Music by RICHARD RODGERS

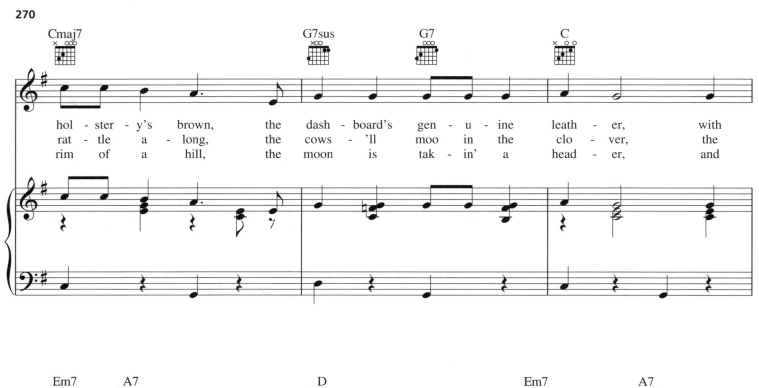

hol - ster - y's brown, the dash - board's gen - u - ine leath - er, with
rat - tle a - long, the cows - 'll moo in the clo - ver, the
rim of a hill, the moon is tak - in' a head - er, and

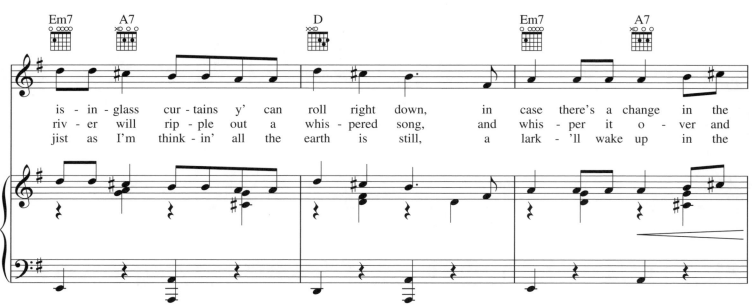

is - in - glass cur - tains y' can roll right down, in case there's a change in the
riv - er will rip - ple out a whis - pered song, and whis - per it o - ver and
jist as I'm think - in' all the earth is still, a lark - 'll wake up in the

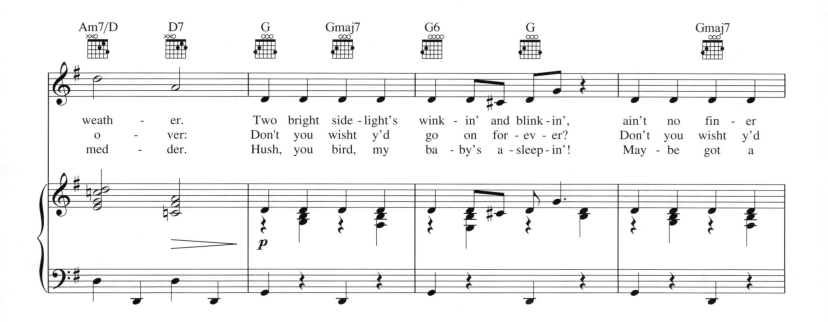

weath - er. Two bright side - light's wink - in' and blink - in', ain't no fin - er
o - ver: Don't you wisht y'd go on for - ev - er? Don't you wisht y'd
med - der. Hush, you bird, my ba - by's a - sleep - in'! May - be got a

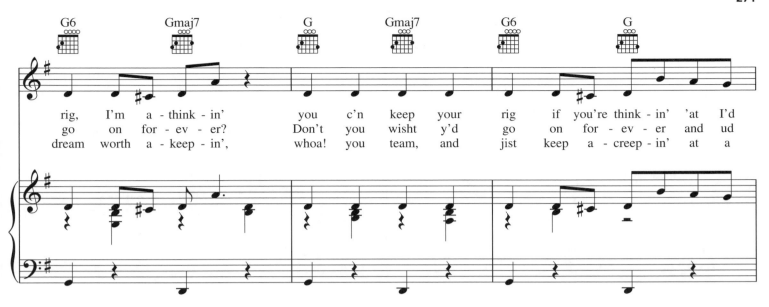

rig, I'm a-think-in'   you c'n keep your rig if you're think-in' 'at I'd
go   on for-ev-er?   Don't you wisht y'd go   on for-ev-er and ud
dream worth a-keep-in',   whoa! you team, and jist keep a-creep-in' at   a

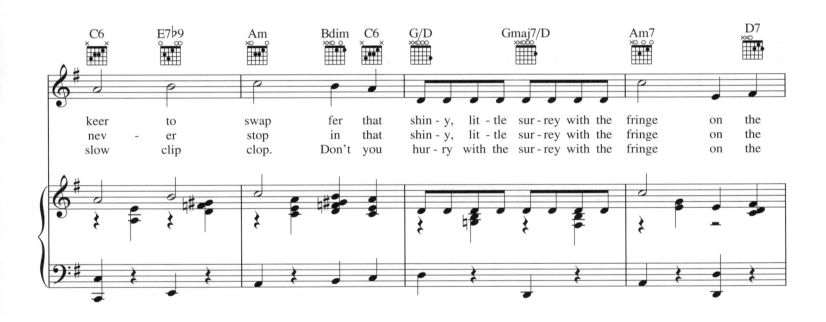

keer   to   swap   fer that shin-y, lit-tle sur-rey with the fringe on the
nev - er   stop   in   that shin-y, lit-tle sur-rey with the fringe on the
slow   clip   clop.   Don't you hur-ry with the sur-rey with the fringe on the

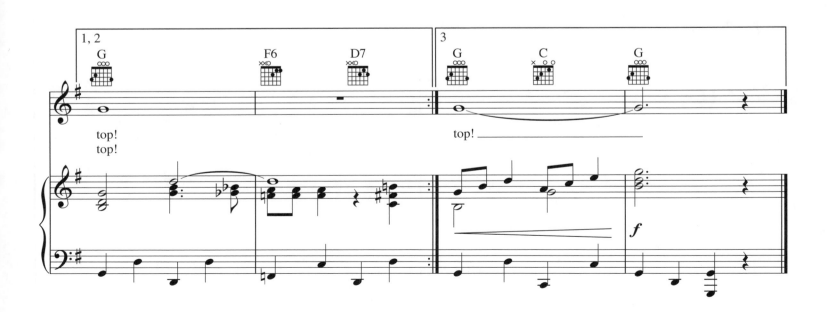

top!
top!   top!

THE SWEETEST SOUNDS

from NO STRINGS

Lyrics and Music by
RICHARD RODGERS

THEY CALL THE WIND MARIA

from PAINT YOUR WAGON

Words by ALAN JAY LERNER
Music by FREDERICK LOEWE

THANK HEAVEN FOR LITTLE GIRLS

from GIGI

Words by ALAN JAY LERNER
Music by FREDERICK LOEWE

THAT FACE
from THE PRODUCERS

Music and Lyrics by
MEL BROOKS

THERE'S A SMALL HOTEL

from ON YOUR TOES

Words by LORENZ HART
Music by RICHARD RODGERS

THERE'S NO BUSINESS LIKE SHOW BUSINESS

from the Stage Production ANNIE GET YOUR GUN

Words and Music by
IRVING BERLIN

The butch - er the bak - er, the
The cos - tumes, the scen - 'ry, the
The cow - boys, the tum - blers, the

gro - cer, the clerk are se - cret - ly un -
make - up, the props, the au - di - ence that
wrest - lers, the clowns, the roust - a - bouts who

295

THIS CAN'T BE LOVE
from THE BOYS FROM SYRACUSE

Words by LORENZ HART
Music by RICHARD RODGERS

THOROUGHLY MODERN MILLIE

from THOROUGHLY MODERN MILLIE

Words by SAMMY CAHN
Music by JAMES VAN HEUSEN

TOGETHER WHEREVER WE GO

from GYPSY

Words by STEPHEN SONDHEIM
Music by JULE STYNE

WHEN I'M NOT NEAR
THE GIRL I LOVE
from FINIAN'S RAINBOW

Words by E.Y. HARBURG
Music by BURTON LANE

313

TRY TO REMEMBER
from THE FANTASTICKS

Words by TOM JONES
Music by HARVEY SCHMIDT

WE KISS IN A SHADOW

from THE KING AND I

Lyrics by OSCAR HAMMERSTEIN II
Music by RICHARD RODGERS

C F E D7 E7
sigh For one smil - ing day to be
cresc.
Am C7 F
free To kiss in the
mf
p legato
C7
sun - light And say to the sky
7
N.C. F13
Be - hold and be - lieve what you see!

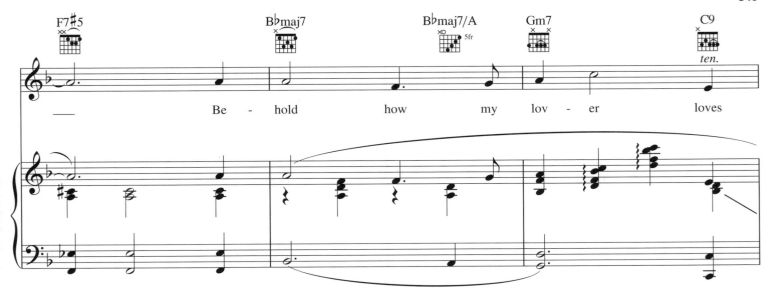

Be - hold how my lov - er loves

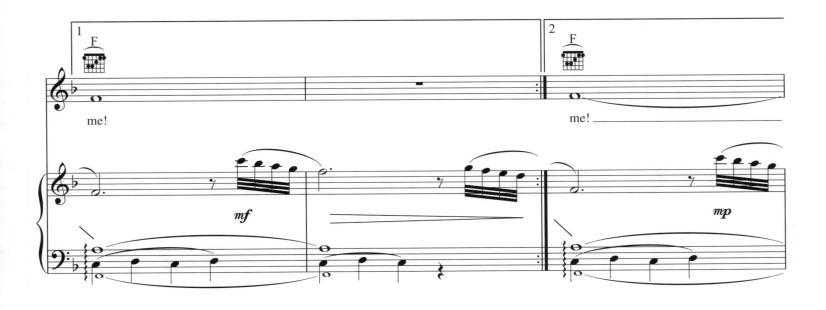

me!   me!

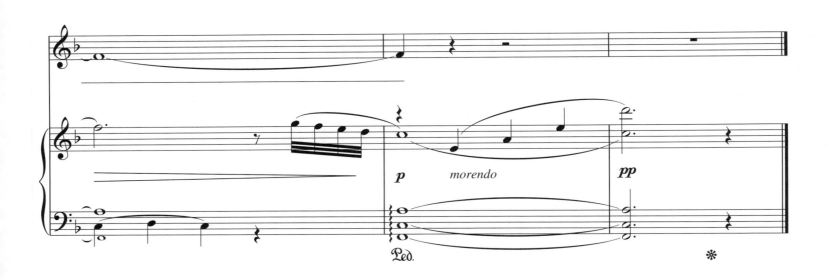

WHAT KIND OF FOOL AM I?

from the Musical Production STOP THE WORLD—I WANT TO GET OFF

Words and Music by LESLIE BRICUSSE
and ANTHONY NEWLEY

WHERE OR WHEN

from BABES IN ARMS

Words by LORENZ HART
Music by RICHARD RODGERS

WITHOUT LOVE
from HAIRSPRAY

Music by MARC SHAIMAN
Lyrics by MARC SHAIMAN and SCOTT WITTMAN

Once I was a self-ish fool who nev-er un-der-stood. I

nev-er looked in-side my-self, though on the out-side, I looked good!

I'll be yours for-ev - er 'cause I nev-er wan - na be with-out

love. So Dar - ling, nev - er set me

free. I'm yours for-ev - er. Nev-er set me

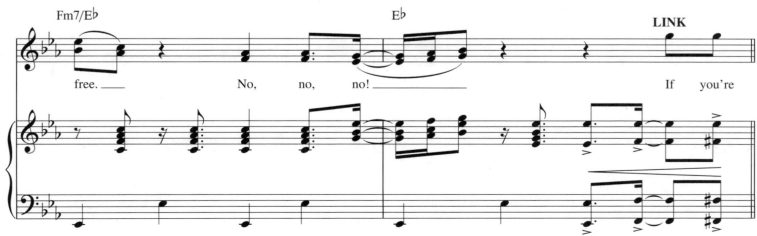

free. No, no, no! If you're

337

WHO CAN I TURN TO
(When Nobody Needs Me)
from THE ROAR OF THE GREASEPAINT—THE SMELL OF THE CROWD

Words and Music by LESLIE BRICUSSE
and ANTHONY NEWLEY

339

WISH YOU WERE HERE

from WISH YOU WERE HERE

Words and Music by
HAROLD ROME

A WONDERFUL DAY LIKE TODAY

from THE ROAR OF THE GREASEPAINT—THE SMELL OF THE CROWD

Words and Music by LESLIE BRICUSSE
and ANTHONY NEWLEY

YOU RULE MY WORLD

from THE FULL MONTY

Words and Music by
DAVID YAZBEK

351

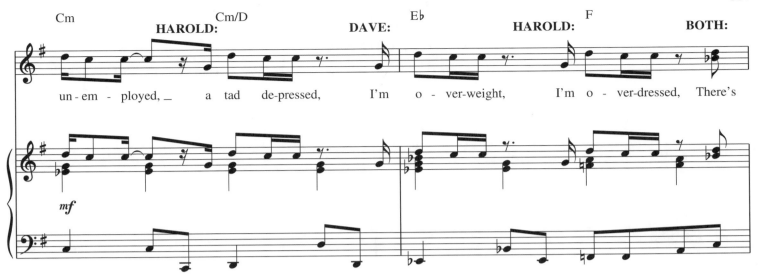

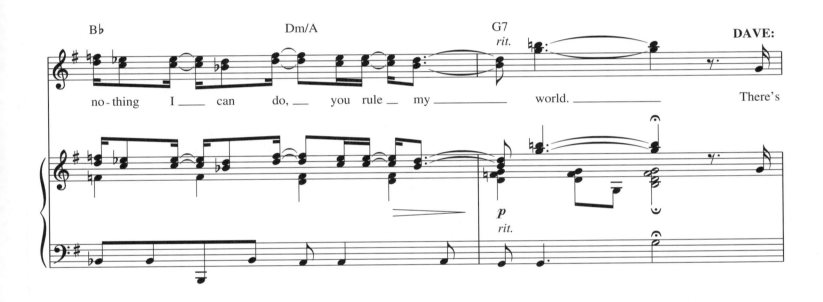

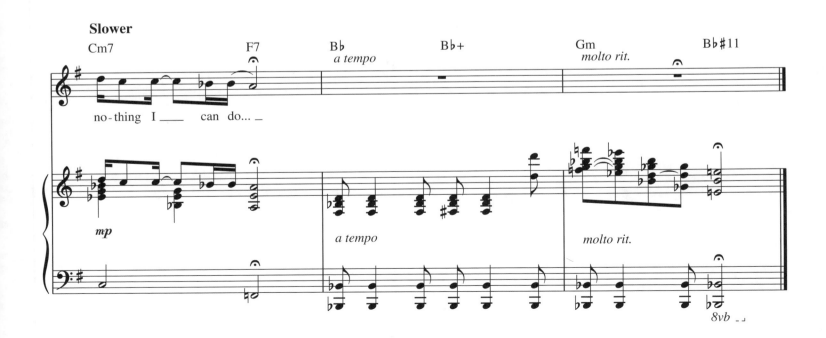

A WONDERFUL GUY

from SOUTH PACIFIC

Lyrics by OSCAR HAMMERSTEIN II
Music by RICHARD RODGERS

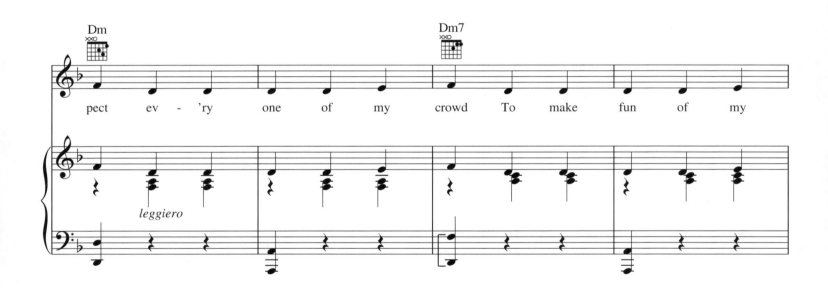

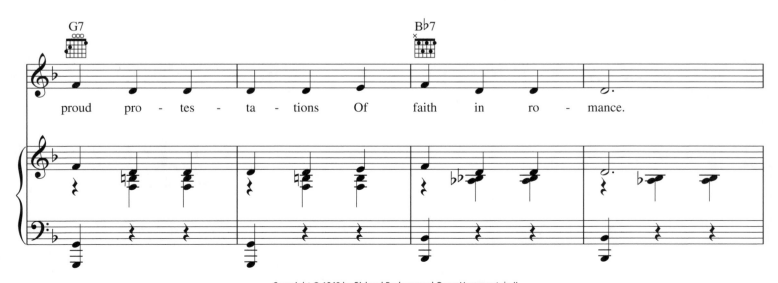

Fear - less - ly I'll face them and ar - gue their doubts a - way.

WOULDN'T IT BE LOVERLY

from MY FAIR LADY

Words by ALAN JAY LERNER
Music by FREDERICK LOEWE

363

WRITTEN IN THE STARS

from Walt Disney Theatrical Productions' AIDA

Music by ELTON JOHN
Lyrics by TIM RICE

I am here to tell you we can nev-er meet a-gain

Sim-ple real-ly is-n't it? ___ A word or two ___ and then a

life-time of not know-ing where or how ___ or why ___ or when ___ You

366

367

WUNDERBAR

from KISS ME, KATE

Words and Music by
COLE PORTER

YOU ARE BEAUTIFUL

from FLOWER DRUM SONG

Lyrics by OSCAR HAMMERSTEIN II
Music by RICHARD RODGERS

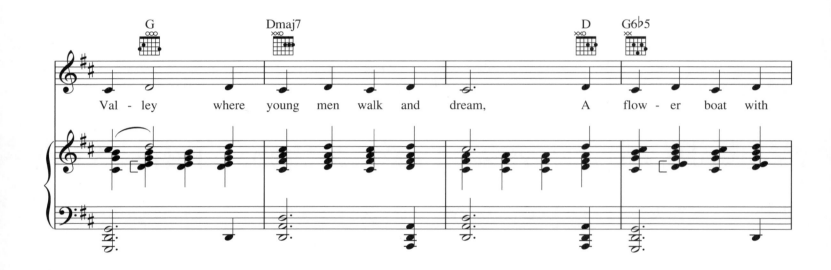

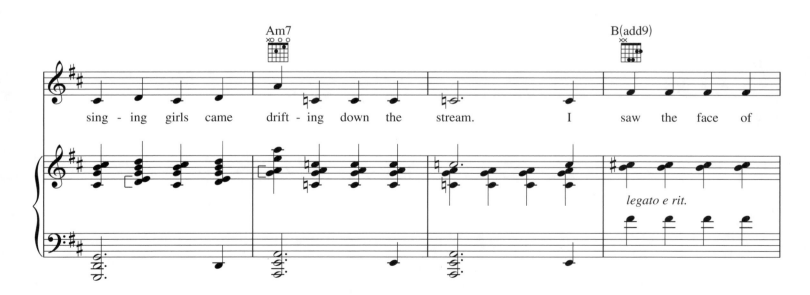

on - ly one come drift - ing down the stream.

più rit. *a tempo* *mp*

Refrain *(tranquillo)*

You are beau - ti - ful, small and shy.

p dolce

You are the girl whose eyes met mine Just as your boat sailed

by. This I know of you,

YOU'D BE SO NICE TO COME HOME TO

from SOMETHING TO SHOUT ABOUT

Words and Music by
COLE PORTER

YOUNGER THAN SPRINGTIME

from SOUTH PACIFIC

Lyrics by OSCAR HAMMERSTEIN II
Music by RICHARD RODGERS

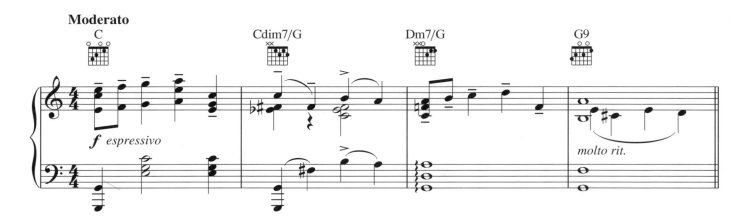

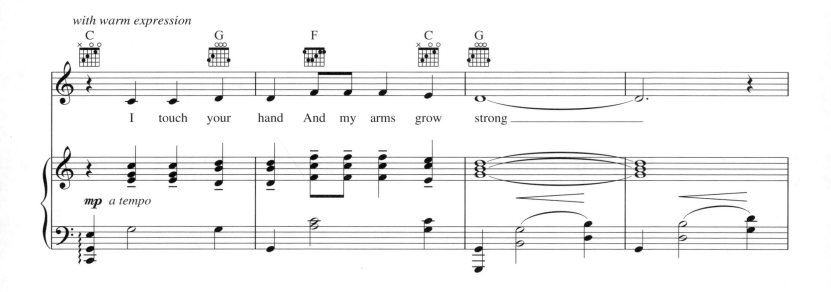

I touch your hand And my arms grow strong _____

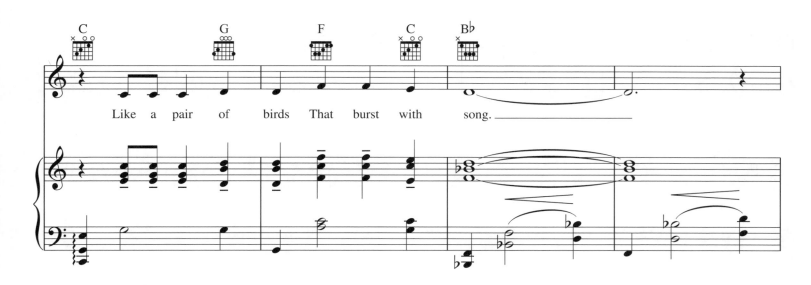

Like a pair of birds That burst with song. _____

YOU'LL NEVER WALK ALONE

from CAROUSEL

Lyrics by OSCAR HAMMERSTEIN II
Music by RICHARD RODGERS

Andantino molto cantabile

(with great warmth, like a hymn)

When you walk through a storm, *keep your chin up high And don't be a-fraid of the dark, _____ At the end of the

* alternate lyric: hold your head up high